CONFUSED D

CHILLING TALES ACTIVITY BOOK

BEFORE, DURING, & AFTER READING ACTIVITIES FOR TWO SPINE-CHILLING STORIES

TO OUR AWESOME READERS -

HAPPY HOLIDAYS!
-THE CONFUSED DUDES

DON'T FORGET TO STAY SPOOKY!

STORY 1: BEFORE READING ACTIVITIES

1. Do you enjoy the cold weather? Why or why not? What type of weather do you enjoy the most?

----

2. Identify your favorite activity to do when it snows! Go sledding? Drink hot chocolate? Build a snowman?

BEFORE READING ACTIVITIES

FOCUS ON VOCABULARY

What do you think the word "sinister" means? Read the following sentence. Then, use context clues to jot down possible meanings.

To make our house look <u>sinister</u> for Halloween, we decorated the outside with cobwebs, tombstones, and ghosts!

Possible meaning of "sinister"

_____

_____

_____

Now that you've thought about the definition, use a separate piece of paper to draw a

SINISTER HAUNTED HOUSE!

STORY 1: DURING READING ACTIVITIES

ANSWER THESE QUESTIONS AS YOU ARE READING "CONFUSED DUDES AND THE SINISTER SNOWMAN!"

1. Make an inference! Why do DJ and Parker "plop" their wet boots on a towel? Have you ever been told to do this? (First page)

----

2. Predict how the shining sun may affect the snowman. Share your ideas. (First page)

3. Why do DJ and Parker think the snowman looks sinister? (Third page)

----

4. Have you ever heard the phrase "the proof is in the pudding?" What do YOU think it means? (Sixth page)

CONFUSED DUDES AND THE SINISTER SNOWMAN

"EPIC SNOW DAY!" Parker burst through the door.

"Dude! I can't believe how much it snowed overnight! It's SNOWMAN TIME!"

Joyfully, DJ and Parker trailed through the snow.

After creating a snowman shape and designing the face, Parker placed a creepy hat right on top.

"The final piece to our awesome snow dude!"

The boys shuffled back to the kitchen. They plopped their wet boots on a towel and sipped on hot chocolate. Two hours later, the two returned outside. The sun was shining brightly.

"It's not as cold," DJ observed.

"Hey **MR. SNOW DUDE**!" Parker called.

He frowned. "The snow dude looks different."

DJ scratched his head. "He looks skinny!"

"Cookies are done!" DJ's mom declared from the kitchen.

"Later, **MR. SNOW DUDE**!" Parker yelled.

As the boys devoured cookies, Juliet strolled into the kitchen.

"The rest are all yours, sis! We need to go back outside to check on our snow dude. He looked skinnier before. How does he look now?"

Juliet peered outside.

"The proof is in the pudding!" she declared, as she chomped on cookies and left the kitchen.

Parker rushed to the window and gasped.

The snow dude had holes where there was once glistening snow. It was almost as if he had BONES! Even worse, his face seemed to have a CREEPY GRIN!

"The snow dude looks like a SKELETON!"

DJ's eyes scanned the room. "I don't think **MR. SNOW DUDE** is a jolly snowman. I think we've created –

A SINISTER SNOWMAN!"

Parker shuddered. "What do sinister snowmen do?"

"Lots of creepy things," DJ whispered.

"Steal your dreidel, kidnap an elf, totally CREEP OUT Santa!"

Parker panicked. "We can't let the sinister snowman ruin the holidays!"

DJ paced the kitchen. "Juliet said the proof was in the pudding. My dad made some rice pudding last night."

"You think the answer is in *there*?" Parker questioned.

"It's worth a try! Maybe covering the snow dude in rice pudding will stop him."

"Anything to save the holidays!" Parker shouted.

DJ and Parker were leaving the kitchen with a giant bowl of rice pudding when Juliet spotted them.

"What are you dudes doing?" she asked.

The boys stuttered.

"The snow dude!"

"He's sinister!"

"HE'LL TOTALLY CREEP OUT SANTA!"

"I'm confused," Juliet said.

"You said the answer was in the pudding," DJ explained.

Juliet burst into laughter.

"Listen up, confused dudes. You won't find any answers in that pudding. And the snowman isn't going to totally creep out Santa."

Juliet pointed to the window. "Look outside – the sun is shining! So, your snow dude," she giggled, "is melting, of course."

"The proof is in the pudding is called an idiom. An idiom is a statement NOT to be taken literally. The statement means to look at the results to get your answer. The sun was clearly causing the snowman to melt and change shape."

"DJ, what did mom say yesterday when it was raining?"

"It's raining cats and dogs!" he shouted.

"Great! Parker, what did your dad tell you before the science fair?"

"Break a leg!" he shouted.

"Awesome sauce!"

"Juliet, how about we don't mention this mix-up to mom and dad? Dad would have been crushed if we wasted all his rice pudding," DJ said.

Juliet put her arms around the two buddies. "You got it, spooky dudes. Count on me

NOT TO SPILL THE BEANS!"

STORY 1: AFTER READING ACTIVITIES

STEM ACTIVITIES

Use a computer to find the answers to these questions about **SNOWFLAKES**! Need help? Ask a friend, parent, teacher, or sibling!

1. Snowflakes are formed from ice crystals. How many ice crystals are typically in a snowflake?

_____

2. How many sides does a snowflake have?

_____

3. Why are snowflakes drinkable?

_____

_____

_____

_____

4. According to the Guinness World Records, how big was the largest recorded snowflake?

_____

5. Now, grab a paper plate if you have one! If not, paper is just fine. Design the most interesting snowflake you can imagine!

DESIGN A CREEPY SNOWMAN

WILL YOUR SNOWMAN HAVE A CROOKED CARROT NOSE?

A SINISTER SMILE?

A HORRIFYING HAT?

BATS FOR EYES INSTEAD OF BUTTONS?

A SCARF MADE OF SNAKES?

STORY 2: BEFORE READING ACTIVITIES

1. Do you like spiders? Why or why not? Do you find them cool? Boring? Terrifying?

----

2. Describe what you think would be the PERFECT sleepover!

BEFORE READING ACTIVITIES
FOCUS ON VOCABULARY

What do you think the word "inspiration" means? Read the following sentence. Then, use context clues to jot down possible meanings.

In the story, Juliet states, *"It's the perfect setting for a spooky scene. The dark, the dust, the creepy noises – think of the inspiration!"*

Possible meaning of "inspiration"

_____

_____

_____

Now that you've thought about the definition, use a separate piece of paper to draw something that INSPIRES YOU!

CONFUSED DUDES & THE CREEPY BUG HUG

"FRIDAY SLEEPOVER!" Parker burst through the door. "BRRR, it's cold out there!" He shivered.

"SPOOKY Friday sleepover!" DJ added.
Juliet strolled into the living room with her friend Hazel.

"Hey, SPOOKY DUDES! Hazel is sleeping over tonight, too. I know how late you stay up telling scary stories. And how loud you can be. How about sleeping in the basement tonight?"

DJ shrugged.

"Think about it! It's the perfect setting for a spooky scene. The dark, the dust, the creepy noises – think of the INSPIRATION!"

The boys nodded. "Okay, Juliet!"

"Great! One more thing – there are a million SPIDERS down there. Cool, huh? Later, gators!"

"A million," Parker whispered.

"Spiders," DJ finished.

"I don't know about this. Maybe we should sleep in the bathroom!" Parker began to panic.

"Remain calm, dude. I have a plan. There are spider books in my room."

Parker nodded slowly. "And if we learn some facts about spiders, maybe it won't seem so bad."

Back in DJ's room, the boys read the first spider book they could find.

Suddenly, Parker gasped. "Dude, it says here that most spiders have EIGHT eyes! If there are a million spiders down there, that means," he quickly counted on his fingers, "billions and billions of **EYEBALLS** on us!"

DJ shuddered. "Billions of **EYEBALLS** on us ALL night!"

"Waiting until we fall asleep," Parker whispered.

"What if there's a queen spider?" DJ continued "You know - like with bees!"

"What if she has even MORE **EYEBALLS**?" Parker trembled.

DJ threw his book on the floor. "Dude, we are spooky experts. Maybe we can sneak our sleeping bags down there. The basement has a separate room in the back."

"Sneak in that back room? But how? All those **EYEBALLS** on us?" Parker pulled DJ's blanket up to his chin.

"If I grab our sleeping bags," DJ said, "I can sneak them into that back room. You can go down there first."

"What am I going to do?" Parker asked.

"What if you cover their **EYEBALLS**?" DJ suggested. "Then, they won't see where I'm bringing our sleeping bags. And, spiders are small, right? Think of it as," he paused and finally declared, "a hug!"

Parker frowned. "A hug?"

"Yeah, a creepy bug hug! That's all. And creepy dudes need love, too - right?"

During Reading Question:
What would YOU do if you were Parker?

Parker sighed. "I'm not happy about this dude, but I guess I'll give it a try."

An hour later, Parker and DJ tiptoed to the basement door. DJ was carrying the sleeping bags.

Parker wore a snowsuit.

Juliet and Hazel spotted the boys.

"What are you dudes doing?" Juliet asked.

The boys stuttered.

"You said there were a million SPIDERS down here," DJ started.

"And that means billions of EYEBALLS!" Parker finished.

"And the snowsuit can protect Parker from the creepy bug hug," DJ stammered.

Juliet and Hazel burst into laughter.

"Listen up, confused dudes. There aren't really a million spiders in the basement. I was simply using a hyperbole. A hyperbole is an exaggeration. For example, my backpack weighs a ton!"

"DJ - now you try it!"

"Mom told me a million times to clean my room!" he shouted.

"Awesome, bro! Parker - how about you?"

"It must be a thousand degrees in this snowsuit," he groaned.

"Nailed it, spooky dudes!"

"Besides," Hazel said, "spiders are awesome. Did you know that spiders create silk to make webs? Or that some spiders can change color?

"Wow," the boys whispered.

"DJ, are you sure you're both okay with sleeping in the basement?" Juliet asked.

"Are we? Absolutely! In fact, we might just hang with those

COOL DUDES FOREVER."

STORY 2: AFTER READING ACTIVITIES

Let's practice using hyperboles! See if you can fill in the blanks using an exaggeration.

FOCUS ON HYPERBOLE

1. The boy cried a _____ when his bike was stolen.

2. The puppy is as skinny as a _____.

3. I tried to solve that math problem _____ times!

4. Have you seen her play soccer? She can run as fast as a _____.

5. The candy store had _____ lollipops!

6. I'm so hungry I could eat _____!

Some of these hyperboles are also similes! A simile is a comparison between two unalike objects using "like" or "as." Give the next worksheet a try!

SNOW AND SIMILES

1 THIS SNOW IS AS COLD AS _____.

2. My dog ran like _____ through the slushy sleet.

3. FINDING TWO IDENTICAL SNOWFLAKES IS AS RARE AS _____.

4. The newly fallen snow covered the lawn like a _____.

5. EVEN IN SOCKS. MY TOES ARE AS COLD AS _____.

6. THE FRIGID WIND LEFT MY CHEEKS AS RED AS _____.

MEET THE AUTHOR

Cristina Worgul is a high school English teacher from Long Island, New York. She lives with her husband, three children, and two rambunctious puppies.

Cristina is also the author of "Confused Dudes and the Sockness Monster" and "Confused Dudes and Haunted Hazel."

MEET THE ILLUSTRATOR

Andrew Traficante is an award-winning Manhattan local graphic designer whose passion has always been art.

Originally born on Long Island, he established his own caricature entertainment business, occupying the entire New York state with his talent under the name Drew'z Cartoonz.

Born in October, he has always had an interest in horror. Aside from drawing, he was an elite-wrestler who enjoys skateboarding and extreme sports.